Lisa Bean Goldman

The Proud Little Burro

by Lisa Bear Goldman

with illustrations by Patrice Schooley

Buddy and his best friend, Diego, ran in circles around the far end of the corral. This was Buddy's favorite game. He made a quick and sharp turn, kicking up his heels and throwing as much dirt into the air as he could.

Buddy brayed happily when a cloud of dirt rose high into the sky. Buddy was smaller than Diego but he knew he could send dirt clods flying as high as any mule could send them into the air.

Out of the corner of his eye he saw the head wrangler walking toward the corral. Buddy stopped and saw that all the other animals were watching, as well. Buddy and Diego joined the herd and waited. They all wanted to know what jobs they would be given.

Raven flew by and loudly announced herself, as she so often did. Buddy had heard his mother tell the story that Raven brought the sun to all creatures. Buddy didn't know if this was true but he always liked to see the sun reflecting off her.

Raven landed on a post near Buddy's head. She was so close he could see every color of the rainbow in her feathers.

Raven winked at him. She was well known for her sense of humor and playful nature.

The wrangler opened the gate to the corral with a halter in his hand, and walked over to one of the older mules. This usually meant a few animals from the herd would be picked to go on a trip along the desert trails into the red stone canyon. Even though he had gotten used to being handled and carrying things on his back, Buddy had never been chosen for a real journey. He was hoping this might be his time to go.

One by one the mules and burros were led out of the corral and tied to the hitching rails. Buddy knew he was young, but he had grown a little and he was sure he was strong enough now. He had heard so many tales of exciting adventures from these trips and Buddy was tired of being left behind. Buddy watched Diego stand patiently as a halter was placed on his head and he was led out to a hitching post. Diego had gone on several trips already.

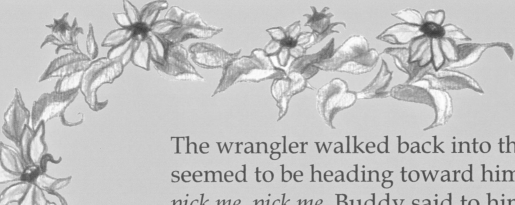

The wrangler walked back into the corral and seemed to be heading toward him. *Pick me, pick me, pick me*, Buddy said to himself. Was he finally going to get to go? Buddy held his breath and his heart pounded.

The wrangler stopped next to him and Buddy stood as tall as he could, pushing his ears to the sky. He took deep breaths to make his chest as big and wide as he could.

Over his shoulder he saw Raven sitting on the fence. She was hooting her laughter. Buddy ignored her calls. When he felt the halter placed over his nose, Buddy wanted to sing. As he was led out of the corral, he felt he was walking on air. All eyes were on him. Buddy felt so grown up and so very proud.

Diego was tied next to him. Buddy watched as a saddle was placed on Diego's back and then tightened around his chest. Diego would carry a person on their trip and he stood tall knowing his job was an important one.

Buddy waited his turn, but his heart sank when he saw the wooden frame used for the pack animals, brought over to him. The rough frame was strapped onto his back and then two heavy bags were tied to the sides of the pack frame.

Buddy knew he was strong and could carry the load but he felt embarrassed. He tried to hide his disappointment. This was not the job he wanted. He thought he would be carrying a handsome saddle and a person.

Where was the honor in carrying lumpy bags filled with packages, he asked himself? Buddy hung his head and would not look at his friend, Diego.

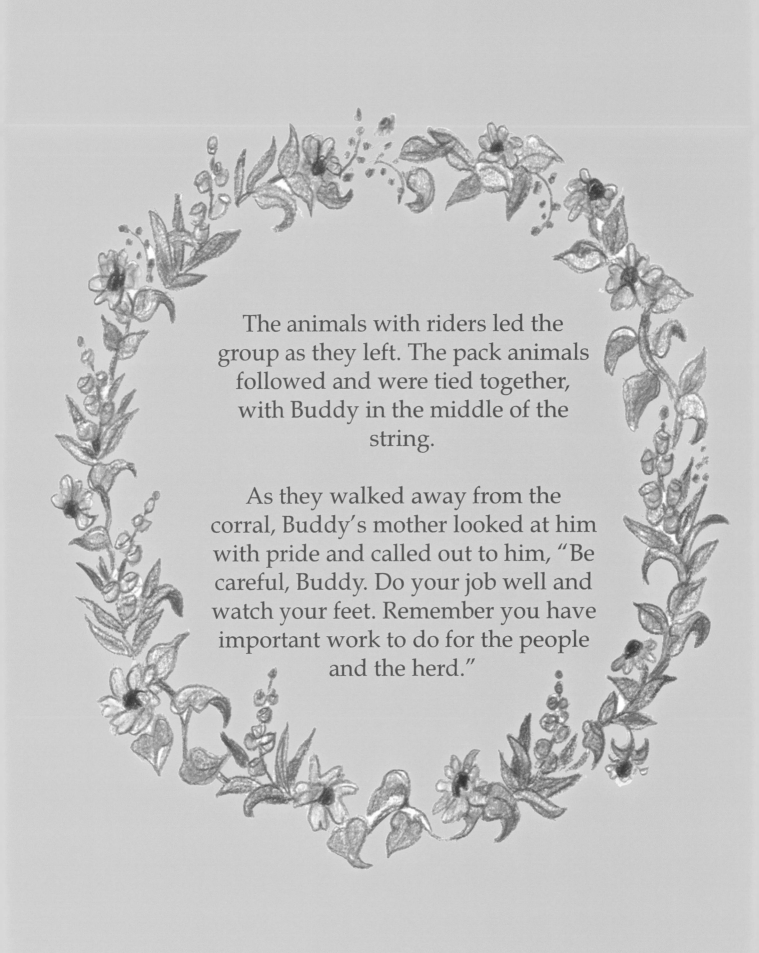

The animals with riders led the group as they left. The pack animals followed and were tied together, with Buddy in the middle of the string.

As they walked away from the corral, Buddy's mother looked at him with pride and called out to him, "Be careful, Buddy. Do your job well and watch your feet. Remember you have important work to do for the people and the herd."

Buddy did not raise his head as he walked by her. He felt ashamed of the ugly bags strapped to his back.

Buddy worked hard. His load was heavy and he had to watch
for the big jagged rocks as he placed his feet carefully on the
trail. Sometimes the trail crossed the sandy and dry arroyo
at the bottom of the canyon. Raven flew nearby. She seemed
to be following them. Several times the entire group stopped
and Buddy was happy for the chance to rest. Whenever they
stopped, the people got out of their saddles and walked up to
the rock walls of the canyon.

They would stare in silence at scratches on the rocks and then speak excitedly. Buddy could see when he walked by the rocks that there were pictures of people, animals and strange designs on the cliff face. If he could just stop wishing he had a saddle and a person on his back, he could feel happy.

The string of people and animals went deeper and deeper into the canyon.

All of a sudden, Buddy was startled to hear one of the people yelling on the trail ahead of him. He did not know what all the commotion was about, but now all of the animals were stopped. He waited with the others and then he heard the news. Diego was hurt. A piece of glass, hidden in soft sand had sliced his leg, and he was bleeding.

Suddenly, the head wrangler came running down the trail toward him. He stopped at Buddy's side and untied one of the saddle bags. With quick moving hands he unwrapped medical supplies. Buddy watched the wrangler then carry a first aid kit up toward Diego. Now Buddy was really worried.

Raven sat on a rock and Buddy asked her to please tell Diego he was his best friend and he loved him. He wanted to help Diego in some way. Raven nodded, winked at him and flew off.

It seemed to take forever, but Buddy finally saw one of the wranglers leading Diego down the trail toward him. Diego's leg was wrapped in bandages and he was limping.

His friend was walking, though, and Buddy let out a big sigh. When Diego passed him they touched noses and shared a breath. Buddy watched him walk down the trail toward home and he felt certain Diego would be all right.

The head wrangler made his way back to Buddy and wrapped the first aid supplies back into a bundle. He gave Buddy a pat on the neck. The other animals nodded their approval and Buddy's chest swelled with pride.

He now understood the packages he carried on his back were very important. The wrangler strapped the big saddle bags back onto Buddy's pack frame.

Raven winked again, and she called to him as she flew away, "I will tell your mother you are holding your head high again, Little Buddy."

Even though he knew she teased him, Raven's words felt like the glorious warmth of the sun shining on him.

While Buddy's back was sore and his legs tired as daylight faded, his spirit was happy. He remembered his mother's words that morning and Buddy now understood what she'd meant when she'd said his job was important to the people and to his herd.

The next morning Buddy stood proudly as his pack frame and bags were tied onto his back.

On the trail he held his head high and felt so good he wished he could run and kick clods of dirt into the air.

Instead he tossed his head and smiled from the inside out.

The End

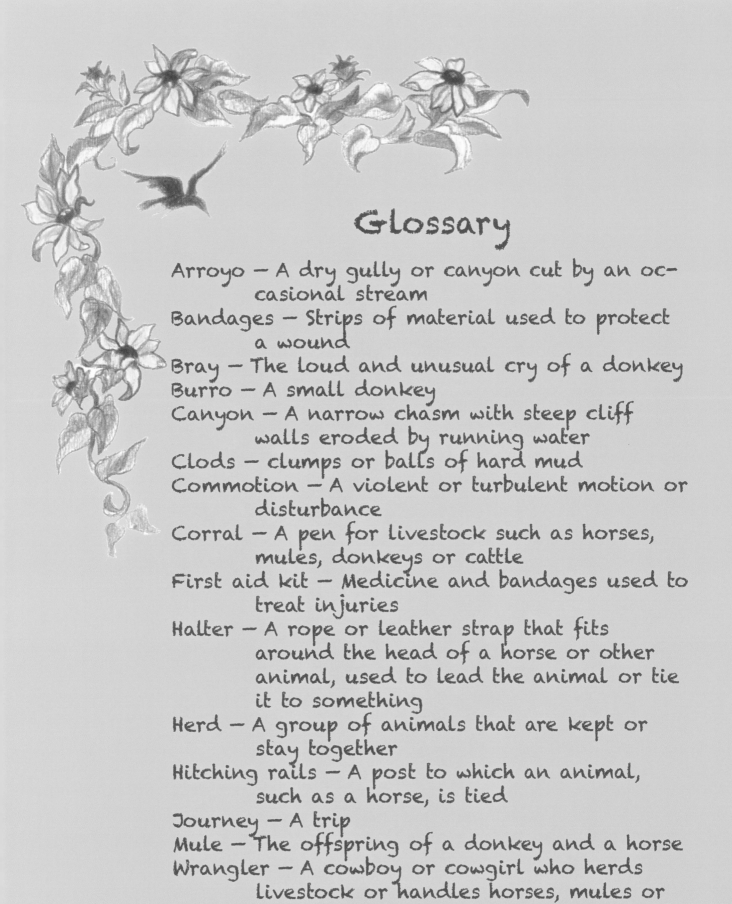

Glossary

Arroyo — A dry gully or canyon cut by an occasional stream

Bandages — Strips of material used to protect a wound

Bray — The loud and unusual cry of a donkey

Burro — A small donkey

Canyon — A narrow chasm with steep cliff walls eroded by running water

Clods — clumps or balls of hard mud

Commotion — A violent or turbulent motion or disturbance

Corral — A pen for livestock such as horses, mules, donkeys or cattle

First aid kit — Medicine and bandages used to treat injuries

Halter — A rope or leather strap that fits around the head of a horse or other animal, used to lead the animal or tie it to something

Herd — A group of animals that are kept or stay together

Hitching rails — A post to which an animal, such as a horse, is tied

Journey — A trip

Mule — The offspring of a donkey and a horse

Wrangler — A cowboy or cowgirl who herds livestock or handles horses, mules or donkeys.

Burrito poses with his author and illustrator. He is very proud
to have been the inspiration for this story and the model
for Buddy. His best friends and dear companions are
two horses—Bill and Beau. He is glad to have found
his forever home in the mountains of Placitas, NM,
where he is loved and appreciated
for being his cute 300 lb. self.

Lisa Bear Goldman is a published children's book author and a counselor. She spent her early years in Albuquerque and Santa Fe, New Mexico, and then attended the University of Arizona, in Tucson, Arizona, where she completed her Master's Degree in Rehabilitation Counseling. She currently works as a counselor in New Mexico. In addition to her love of writing, she works as an artist's representative for her father, Herb Goldman, an accomplished sculptor. Lisa is on the Board of Directors of Art Has Heart, JB & Amado Pena's foundation providing educational scholarships for young people. Lisa's work as a counselor inspired her to write The Proud Little Burro. She wanted to encourage children to take pride in any job that they choose to do. She has a miniature donkey, who was the model for the illustrations this book.

After receiving a Fine Arts Degree from the University of New Mexico, Patrice Schooley began doing juried shows with her watercolors, acrylics and pencil art. Eventually she found her true passion in painting animals and children and has done commissioned work throughout the United States. Patrice believes in the importance of art for children and has taught many classes both in the schools and in private lessons. She also devotes much of her time to animal rescue work and always donates a portion of her sales to various animal charities. She recently was accepted as a member of Art Helping Animals, an international group of artists whose mission it is to help animals through their art. Patrice believes that all animals have many wonderful and magical things to teach humans if we take the time to listen. She was delighted to have been able to work with a real donkey as her model and muse for the illustrations for this book.

Library of Congress Control Number: 2011927137

ISBN 978-0-9832074-0-5 (pbk. : alk. paper)

CPSIA information can be obtained
at www.ICGtesting.com
233189LV00002B